Original title:
Wildflower Whimsy

Copyright © 2025 Creative Arts Management OÜ
All rights reserved.

Author: Clara Whitfield
ISBN HARDBACK: 978-1-80566-613-4
ISBN PAPERBACK: 978-1-80566-898-5

The Soft Trill of Nature's Heart

In meadows green where the daisies spin,
The ladybugs waltz with a cheeky grin.
Grass tickles toes, oh what a delight,
Nature's soft whispers, such a playful sight.

Bees wear tiny hats as they zoom on by,
Seeking sweet nectar from blooms way up high.
A squirrel prances, trying to act grand,
While a curious rabbit plans a surprise band.

An Ode to Unruly Growth

A dandelion stands with a pompous flair,
Declaring its rule over no man's land fair.
Beneath a tall oak, mushrooms all dance,
As if they conspired, 'Let's give growth a chance!'

Vines climb the fences with mischievous glee,
Playing hide and seek with the old bumblebee.
Each leaf a rebel, each petal a jest,
Nature's own circus, each day a fest.

The Subtle Magic of Overlooked Flora

A tiny bluebell hosts a tea party right,
Inviting the ants for an evening delight.
They sip on dew drops while sharing strange tales,
Of games played with raindrops on soft leafy trails.

Clover holds secrets beneath its green crown,
With characters that dance, never wearing a frown.
Whimsical wishes float high on a breeze,
While petals engage in risqué little tease.

Color Dances in the Wind

A splash of red tulips in a delightful row,
While yellow sunflowers put on quite the show.
Petals flitter and flutter like laughter in air,
Colors collide in a whimsical affair.

In the sway of the breeze, the greens all giggle,
As butterflies twirl and their wings start to wiggle.
The earth laughs with daisies, oh what a sight,
As the sun dips low, painting day into night.

The Euphoria of Fragile Sprouts

In the meadow, sprouts they play,
Dancing lightly, bright as day.
One says "Look! I'm taller now!"
Another giggles, takes a bow.

They prance along, a merry band,
With tiny shoes made from the sand.
A breeze whispers, they twirl and spin,
Amidst the chaos, joy begins.

A Canvas of Whimsy and Wonder

A painter's brush, in colors bright,
Each petal laughs in sheer delight.
Daffodils wear hats of sun,
While daisies play and skip and run.

The butterflies gossip; such a scene!
Whispers of pollen, sweet and keen.
Grasshoppers chuckle, hop with flair,
In this wild realm, without a care.

Sprightly Encounters in the Green

A squirrel in shades of nutty brown,
Challenges a badger in a crown.
They race around the blooming patch,
With flowers cheering, what a match!

The ladybugs roll dice on leaves,
While beetles plot their autumn heaves.
Amidst the joy, the sun sneaks in,
Nature's grin is sure to win.

The Colorful Mischief of Nature

A dandelion puffs with glee,
Spreading wishes, wild and free.
In the wind, they swirl and dance,
Every seed has found romance.

The clover giggles, oh so sly,
"Pick me, pick me!" they cry, oh my!
But in this playful petal trove,
It's clear that chaos is the grove!

Petals of Playfulness

In a garden where giggles reside,
Bees wear their hats with a quirky slide.
Butterflies munch on cake made of dew,
While daisies play peekaboo, oh so true.

The tulips gossip, sharing their tea,
A potted plant dreams of being free.
With every breeze, they dance around,
Oh, the silly joy that can always be found.

Dance of the Meadow Daisies

Did you see the daisies in their bright attire?
Twisting and twirling as if caught in a choir.
Grassy tunes draw them into a whirl,
While ladybugs join in, giving a twirl.

Their petals tickle each laughing breeze,
As they sing to the bumblebees with ease.
Around and around, they twine and spin,
Making the flowers giggle, what a din!

Secrets in the Sunlit Grove

In the grove where sunlight pranks the trees,
Squirrels steal secrets from whispering leaves.
With acorns in hand, they break into song,
Oh, the jests and jives where they all belong.

Mossy rocks chuckle as they listen near,
To stories of blooms that twirl in cheer.
A wise old owl rolls his eyes with a grin,
As butterflies chatter, oh where to begin?

Whispers of the Blooming Breeze

The breeze carries tales of blossoms so bright,
Who tickle the daisies with sheer delight.
A tulip tries to juggle, oh what a sight,
While the sun sets in hues of pink and white.

Petal fairies giggle, painting the sky,
As clouds play hopscotch, floating up high.
In this garden of laughter, dreams take a flight,
Where the day melts away into charming night.

Curious Bliss in a Floral Reverie

In the garden, bees take a dance,
Pollen swirling in a merry prance.
Tulips giggle, bending low,
As daisies whisper secrets they know.

Butterflies wear polka-dot gowns,
While sunflowers wear frowns and clowns.
Petals bounce like children at play,
In a world where colors sway.

A bumblebee with a dapper hat,
Flirts with a rose, oh what of that?
Cacti chuckle, keeping their cool,
While lilies sing the silliest rule.

Nature's whimsy, what a sight,
In this floral jest, pure delight.
So tune your heart to this sweet scene,
Join the laughter, feel the glee!

When Colors Meet in Serenade

Rainbow blooms in a jolly array,
Tickle the senses in a bright display.
Crickets chirp in playful refrain,
While roses waltz in a light summer rain.

Pansies play peekaboo with the sun,
As marigolds race, calling it fun.
A dandelion whisper with feathery grace,
Scatters wishes all over the place.

Beehives hum and the petals sway,
In this patch where laughter holds sway.
Every hue ready for the show,
As butterflies waltz, all aglow.

Frogs croak rhythms on lily pads,
While poppies chase away the bad.
In a garden, jubilation's the key,
Where nature plays, wild and free!

The Joyride of Nature's Palette

In a field where colors dance,
Bees in shades of yellow prance,
Daisies giggle, laughing loud,
Wearing crowns of dewdrop cloud.

Buttercups play peek-a-boo,
While the breezes whistle too,
Squirrels twirl with acorn hats,
Rabbits bounce in silly spats.

Blossoms bounce in jester hues,
Painted toes in morning dew,
Nature's palette, oh so bright,
Turns a day from wrong to right.

In this chaos, pure delight,
Every pollinator's flight,
With a wink and twirly cheer,
Nature's jesters draw us near.

Radiance in the Untamed Glen

In the glen where shadows play,
Sunlight beams in golden sway,
Thistles dress in rainbow bites,
Sprinkling tints on frolic flights.

Fluffy clouds in giggles pass,
Grasshoppers dance on greenish glass,
With every leap, a pun so fine,
A nature joke, a cheeky line.

Birds wear hats of leafy lace,
Twisting tails in awkward grace,
Their chirps a symphony of glee,
Count the notes—how wild and free!

Unruly blooms in playful groups,
Smiling down at nature's troops,
Who knew the woods could be this fun?
In every shade, a cheerful pun!

Tumbles of Pollen Perfume

A bouncy breeze begins to play,
Casting scents that lead astray,
Pollen clouds create a mess,
Sneezing blooms in sweet distress.

Bumblebees with busy frowns,
Mischief lurking in their gowns,
They tumble down in pollen pools,
Chasing flowers like little fools.

Daffodils in sunny hats,
Chuckle at the pollen spats,
Tickled by the breezy jest,
Nature's laughter, never rest.

Dancing thistles wave hello,
To the bees that steal the show,
A ballet of buzzing tunes,
In the perfume of bright blooms.

Chaotic Beauty of the Untamed

In the wild where mischief brews,
Colors clash in vibrant hues,
Butterflies in frilly shoes,
Twirl through bushes, chase with news.

Frogs in leaps make quite the scene,
Croaking rhythms, oh so keen,
Chasing flies that buzz and dart,
In this chaos, they're the art.

Tangled vines in playful wraps,
Kissing stones with leafy slaps,
Nature's mess, a charming sight,
Turns a frown to pure delight.

Laughter echoes, bees hum loud,
In this ruckus, we're all proud,
Unruly greens and flowery cheers,
Bring us joy throughout the years.

Mischief Among the Blossoms

In the garden, blooms conspire,
Petals giggle, never tire.
Bees in bow ties, dance with flair,
Bouncing bumbles fill the air.

Daisies swap their sunny hats,
Tulips tease the lazy cats.
Butterflies in vibrant prance,
Join the petals in their dance.

Silly weeds plot in a row,
Whisper secrets, soft and low.
Pansies giggle, pink and bright,
Playing tricks till fall of night.

Laughter echoes through the field,
Nature's antics, never sealed.
In this haven, fun's the key,
Blossoms grinning joyfully.

The Elegance of Nature's Laughter

A dandelion wears a crown,
Tickles wind, and spins around.
With a giggle, seeds take flight,
Whirling gently, pure delight.

Poppies wink and blink their eyes,
Sarcastic sighs and playful lies.
Clovers chuckle underfoot,
As rabbits hop in playful pursuit.

Hummingbirds, oh so sly and spry,
Dart and dash like they can fly.
Nature's jesters, joyous and free,
Crafting laughter, it's plain to see.

In this realm of joyous cheer,
Every bloom brings giggles near.
With elegance, the laughter shows,
As the sunlight brightly glows.

Traces of Sunlit Mischief

Sunshine sprinkles color bold,
Petals shimmer, stories told.
Buzzing whispers scatter wide,
Each bright bloom, a secret guide.

Marigolds play hide and seek,
While violets begin to sneak.
Laughter peeks from every leaf,
Nature's joy, beyond belief.

Sassafras and mint conspire,
To weave scents that never tire.
Jokers in this verdant plot,
Reveal mischief, quite a lot.

As twilight falls, colors blend,
Floral giggles never end.
In this dance of light and glee,
Every bloom's a jubilee.

Caverns of Color and Joy

In a meadow, treasures gleam,
Hues of mischief, like a dream.
Lilies laugh with bubble cheeks,
In their mischief, joy just peaks.

Roses wear a playful grin,
While daisies tease with cotton kin.
Sunflowers stretch to catch the light,
Winking at the world so bright.

Violet hues entwined with green,
Nature's canvas, bright and keen.
Every corner, laughter spills,
Creating joy that always thrills.

Through the caverns, laughter flows,
Colorful whispers as it grows.
In this magic, hearts rejoice,
Nature's humor, pure and voice.

Sunshine Spun with Wild Graces

In the park where daisies dance,
Bees are dressed, and ants prance.
Butterflies in tuxedos fly,
While grasshoppers sing lullabies.

Laughter echoes through the trees,
As squirrels juggle, if you please.
The sun plays peek-a-boo all day,
While shadows join the frolic play.

A jester toad hops with flair,
Beneath the bloom, without a care.
Flowers wink with colors bright,
In this world, all seems just right.

So take a step, let worries roam,
Amongst the petals, find your home.
Laugh with nature, join the spree,
In this vibrant jubilee.

Hidden Treasures of the Meadow

In the meadow, secrets hide,
Beneath the thistle, joy and pride.
A caterpillar wears a crown,
While crickets chirp without a frown.

A dandelion makes a wish,
And a snail dreams of a grand swish.
Ladybugs giggle in their spots,
Gathering laughter with their thoughts.

Fluttering friends in jest do play,
As bumblebees buzz night and day.
Found treasures in blades of grass,
Where every moment seems to pass.

So wander through this sunny land,
With silly critters, hand in hand.
Nature's secrets, vast and wide,
In laughter's wonder, we abide.

Gentle Tinkling of Fickle Florets

Tiny bells on stems ring clear,
Fragrant whispers tickle the ear.
A bloom that giggles in the breeze,
While petals sway, they tickle knees.

The sun dips low, flowers yawn,
A sleepy bee starts to fawn.
Pansies plotting mischief, oh!
Playing tricks on the sun's glow.

On a stem, a spider strings,
A web of laughter, joy it brings.
Hopping frogs join in the tune,
As nightfall greets the silver moon.

With each giggle, blooms unfold,
Adventures shared, and stories told.
In this garden, fun's the art,
The gentle tinkle of nature's heart.

The Playful Garden of Nature's Heart

In gardens where the shadows play,
Flowers dance and giggle away.
Tomato plants share silly jokes,
As squash tops tease the wobbly folks.

A bee in glasses sips some tea,
While rabbits bounce in jubilee.
Wind whispers secrets, oh so sweet,
As daisies twirl, this happy feat.

In every corner, joy abounds,
With giddy sounds and merry grounds.
Violet vines stretch with delight,
In this haven, all feels bright.

So let us join in nature's cheer,
With silly blooms, we hold so dear.
Laughter echoes in the sky,
In this playful world, oh my!

Sprightly Smiles of Meadow Folk

In fields so bright, where laughter plays,
The meadow folk dance on sunny days.
With petals in hand, they twirl around,
Painting the air with joy profound.

A gopher grins, a rabbit prances,
While bees in coats take silly chances.
They sip on dew, the sweetest brew,
And wear big hats of sky so blue.

The daisies giggle at the sun's warm glow,
As critters parade in a funny show.
With every bloom, they share a jest,
Nature's punchline—who's the best!

So join the dance, don't be shy,
With flowers around, we'll reach the sky.
Embrace the whimsy, let laughter spark,
In the meadow's heart, we leave our mark.

Reveries in a Sea of Blossom

In a world of hues, where petals dream,
Each thought takes flight on a gentle stream.
Butterflies chuckle as they flit and glide,
With nectar-filled secrets they can't abide.

An ant dons shades, a funky display,
As ladybugs groove in a bright ballet.
They throw a party beneath the trees,
Inviting all bugs, even the bees!

The tulips tease with their vibrant flair,
While dandelions whisper without a care.
With every breeze, giggles are heard,
In this sea of bloom, happiness stirred.

So come take a dip in this colorful bay,
Where laughter and joy play every day.
In reveries vast, let imaginations soar,
For in this flowerland, who could ask for more?

Twinkling Blossoms at Dawn

At the crack of dawn, when the world awakes,
The flowers shake off their sleepy flakes.
Whispers of giggles dance on the breeze,
As morning dew bows to the bustling bees.

A daffodil shouts, 'I'm the brightest today!'
While violets snicker in lavender sway.
The sun peeks through with a cheeky grin,
'Join the fun, let the laughter begin!'

With petals aglow in the soft morning light,
Each bloom is a star, what a beautiful sight.
They wink at the earth, so sprightly and free,
In this garden of joy, come share with me!

So frolic about in this sparkling dawn,
Among twinkling blooms, we'll be reborn.
Let's laugh with the flowers as they blush and beam,
In a silly fairy tale, let's live the dream!

Laidback Ecstasy of Untamed Greens

In a patch of green, where the grass lays thick,
The critters lounge, it's quite the trick.
With frogs on logs and squirrels in trees,
Each day's a party, a breeze-filled tease.

A hedgehog snoozes, hat askew,
While grasshoppers strut, feeling brand new.
With soft sunny rays, they bask and cheer,
In this laidback world, there's nothing to fear.

The daisies all sway, doing soft little jig,
As a wise old owl gives a cheeky gig.
They share tales of old in the shade so cool,
Nature's classroom—oh, isn't it a jewel!

So roll in the grass, let worries flee,
In untamed greens, come dance with me.
Embrace the joy, let your spirit unwind,
In this wild, wondrous world, true peace you'll find.

Spontaneous Blooming Reverie

In the garden, a daisy sneezes,
Saying "Bless you" to a bee that wheezes.
A rogue tulip wears a hat so bright,
It tiptoes left, then takes off in flight.

Pansies giggle, their faces aglow,
Trading secrets only flowers know.
A wayward petal twirls with glee,
Whispers to the breeze, "Come dance with me!"

Haphazardly Growing Joy

A dandelion dreams of a feted slice,
Wishing on wind, that would be nice.
A clumsy sprout with a stuttered lilt,
Dances to rhythms, happiness built.

The cacti chuckle, with arms in the air,
Poking fun at the roses—oh, what a flair!
Bumbling bumblebees swarm in a waltz,
As odd as a cactus at an indoor ball!

Spirited Sways of the Petal Dance

Poppies pirouette, bold and brash,
While lilies giggle, in colorful splashes.
A butterfly stumbles, falls with a grin,
Twirling above, like it's wearing a chin!

Violets yell, "We're the best in show!"
While marigolds cheer with a colorful glow.
The sunflowers gossip in tall, proud lines,
Swaying nicely to nature's designs.

Blush of the Untamed Corners

In the corner, a rogue fern flirts,
With tulips wearing their colorful skirts.
Grinning daisies tease the shy orchids,
"Join us, dear pals, drop all the worries!"

The wind giggles, tickling each leaf,
Frolicking corners, no room for grief.
A daisies' confetti takes to the sky,
While buttercups watch, munching on pie.

Kaleidoscope of Colorful Dreams

In a garden where the daisies dance,
Petals twirl in a dizzying trance.
Bumblebees wear tiny hats,
Sipping nectar, where the giggle sits.

Sunflowers tickle the passing breeze,
Winking at clouds with mischievous ease.
Ladybugs play hopscotch on green,
While grasshoppers flash their grass-stained sheen.

Frogs in bow ties sing out loud,
To the rhythm of a polka crowd.
A butterfly DJ spins in flight,
Turning flowers into a colorful night.

Around the blooms, they twirl and spin,
Chasing shadows where the fun begins.
In this chaos, laughter is found,
Nature's circus, always profound.

Fragments of Floral Free Spirits

A tulip painted with stripes so bold,
Tells secrets of summer tales retold.
Bees in bell-bottoms buzz and sway,
As petals laugh in the afternoon play.

A dandelion makes a wish on air,
While violets giggle without a care.
With each fluff blown across the ground,
New dreams bloom where laughter's found.

The poppies gossip, their whispers sweet,
While wandering cacti tap dance on feet.
Thistles wear crowns, so proudly they rule,
In this patch of fun, they break every rule.

Amidst the blooms, jests blossom free,
A riot of color, a symphony.
Nature's jesters, in a floral spree,
Everything's funny just wait and see!

The Joyful Garden Frolic

In the garden, where the sunbeams play,
Tulips twaddle in a wobbly way.
A humorist bee who tells a joke,
Makes petals giggle until they choke.

The roses are wearing polka-dot pants,
While marigolds join in the silly dance.
Butterflies float like they're on a spree,
Tickling the branches, oh so free.

Wandering weeds with curly hair,
Join the fun without a care.
With laughter bursting from every tree,
The garden's a riot, pure jubilee.

As dusk falls, they hold a ball,
Where all the flowers have fun to enthrall.
In this garden, joy takes the stage,
Every petal turns a glittering page.

Enchanted Fields of Serendipity

In fields where the clovers giggle and tease,
Frolicking foxes dance with the breeze.
Daisies wearing spectacles look so wise,
While winking at clouds in wide-open skies.

A rabbit with dreams of far-off lands,
Draws maps in the dirt with its little hands.
Fields of charm where mischief breeds,
And every flower sprinkles joy like seeds.

Pansies chuckle, a comical bunch,
Making you smile with each silly hunch.
Grass blades whisper the best of jokes,
While deer tap dance, skirting rocks like folks.

Where laughter rings through blooms so bright,
The fields enchant, from morning to night.
In this playful patch of pure delight,
Serendipity glows, a joyful sight.

The Softest Murmurs of Petals

In the breeze, whispers spin,
Dandelions grinning, where to begin?
A bee with a giggle, buzzes near,
Petals are gossiping, oh my dear!

Sun-kissed petals, waving hello,
Come join the party, put on a show!
Butterflies twirl in a silly dance,
Even the leaves join in the trance.

Tickling grasses play peek-a-boo,
With ladybugs hiding, red and blue.
A toad sings high, a comical tune,
Under the watch of a chuckling moon.

Softly they chuckle, rustle, and sway,
In this floral circus, come out and play!
A world of laughter, oh what a sight,
Where petals hold secrets, hidden in light.

Playful Colors in a Sunlit Glade

A splash of red, a dash of blue,
In this glade, mischief brews anew.
Bright hues leap in a lively fight,
Painted by sunbeams, pure delight.

A violet laughs as it tipsy sways,
While daisies romp in a sunlit maze.
Yellow blooms tease, they play coy,
In this garden, there's endless joy.

Colors collide, like kids at play,
Every petal has something to say.
Pink petals tumble, twirl on the breeze,
Nature's giggling, oh please, oh please!

Sunlight giggles, casting bright rays,
While shadows dance in sly, sweet plays.
With each new bloom, a joke is spun,
In this colorful world, we laugh and run.

Secrets Beneath the Canopy

Under the leaves, secrets abound,
With whispers of laughter, funny sounds.
A squirrel in costume, oh what a sight,
Pretending to be a bird, taking flight.

Mushrooms giggle, hiding from eyes,
Telling tall tales of foolish spies.
In this shady nook, hilarity thrives,
With chattering critters, and joyful jives.

Vines twist and turn, in a playful race,
Beneath the branches, they swap silly space.
A rabbit wears glasses, very absurd,
Trying to read a map, have you heard?

Canopy arches, where sunbeams peek,
Nature's comedians share a cheeky tweak.
Mysteries of mischief in the cool shade,
A riot of laughter, no plans laid.

A Serenade of Vibrant Hues

In a garden stage, where colors sing,
Each bloom a jester, ready to fling.
A rose cracks jokes, with petals wide,
As lilacs chuckle, side by side.

Marigolds strut in a golden hue,
Making all the bees laugh, what a crew!
With laughter ringing, they sway to the beat,
A riot of colors, a floral treat.

Petals in a line, like a merry band,
Bringing sunshine, just as they planned.
With every bloom, a new skit unfolds,
In nature's theater, bright stories told.

A riot of hues, a whimsical song,
In this jolly garden, you can't go wrong.
Join in the fun, let your heart race,
In this world of colors, find your place!

The Folly of Nature's Brush

Oh, the daisies tried to dance,
But tripped on grass, oh what a chance!
The tulips blushed, they lost their way,
In a game of prance, they chose to play.

Bees wearing shades buzzed by the blooms,
While butterflies sang in funny tunes.
A sunflower let out a silly grin,
As ants marched past, their tiny kin.

Colors splashed on every leaf,
Painted by laughter, cheeky and brief.
The violets giggled, tumbled around,
As laughter echoed without a sound.

And so we laugh at nature's fun,
In fields of folly, we're all but one.
Join the jest as petals sway,
In this merry dance, we all shall stay.

Whirlwinds of Petal Dreams

The wind made friends with petals bright,
Spinning them round, oh what a sight!
A rose lost its cap and waved goodbye,
While lilacs laughed, oh me, oh my!

Dandelions wore crowns made of fluff,
They said, "We're royalty, just not tough!"
With every gust, they soared so high,
But tumbled down with a cheeky sigh.

The marigolds played peek-a-boo,
As bumblebees joined in too.
With honeyed giggles, they twirled and twirled,
In a whimsical dance, they happily swirled.

Petal dreams rise with each new breeze,
Nature's circus, doing as it please.
With colors bright and spirits high,
We'll laugh along as moments fly.

Echoes of Colorful Secrets

Amid the blooms, secrets unfold,
Whispers of color, stories untold.
The tulips gossip with a wink,
As jade leaves nod and blush at the blink.

Garden gnomes with hats so tall,
Stand guard while petals start to sprawl.
A sunflower reveals a crafty plan,
To prank the weed, oh what a sham!

In shadows deep, the poppies play,
Hiding from bees who buzz all day.
A lilac winked, "We're all in on it!"
As daisies chuckled, they can't ever quit.

In the garden, laughter does ring,
Colorful secrets make hearts take wing.
So join the fun, let spirits be free,
In nature's whim, come play with me!

A Mosaic of Nature's Caprices

In gardens bright, a mosaic sprawls,
With splashes of color that tickle our halls.
Buttercups giggle with each afternoon,
And daisies dance to a playful tune.

Acorn caps are hats for the wise,
While crickets chirp in comical guise.
The wind whispers jokes in tree branches high,
As squirrels throw leaves, oh me, oh my!

Pansies jest, their faces so sly,
While succulents roll their eyes and sigh.
Nature's jokes blossom with every breeze,
In a mosaic crafted with such ease.

So join this dance of capricious cheer,
In vibrant hues, we gather near.
With heart and humor, let's skip along,
In this wild patch of nature's song.

Swaying Colors Underfoot

Amongst the grass the colors dance,
A bluebell's twirl, a daisy's prance.
Each petal giggles, colors tease,
The ground is laughing in the breeze.

With socks so bright, we wade right in,
Our toes are tickled—where to begin?
A patch of yellow leaps to greet,
Hey, don't step here, I'm not a seat!

Lolling in hues, a cheeky gang,
Petals whisper, and the daisies sang.
The world's a flip-flap, vibrant spree,
Come join the dance, it's wild and free.

So pick a spot and let's take aim,
At flowers standing proud, not shy of fame.
The tumbleweeds can watch us glide,
In candied colors, let's abide.

The Melodic Language of Petals

A rose declares, 'Does this smell good?'
While violets blush; oh, how we're all hood!
The lilacs laugh, it's quite the show,
They trade sweet secrets we'll never know!

The tulips flaunt their collars so bright,
With ruffled edges, they feel just right.
Each flower chirps with a tiny chat,
What's that you say? A ladybug sat!

They request a dance, so 'round we go,
With clumsy steps, we steal the show.
Petals flutter, they serenade,
This blooming band's a grand parade!

With wind as our giddy-band leader,
We twirl and skip, just getting sweeter.
A concert of color, chaos, and fun,
In this whimsical garden, we've just begun!

Kaleidoscope of the Untrampled Path

In lands where no foot has dared to tread,
Colors explode like confetti spread.
A pop of pink with a wink of blue,
They giggle together, just me and you!

The honeybees buzz with a chuckle or two,
They're sipping their tea in the morning dew.
Leaves rustle softly, telling tales,
Of bubblegum breezes and butterfly trails.

A dandelion shouts, 'Come blow me around!'
With wishes and dreams, we'll never be bound.
The line is unclear, between here and there,
As we chase the chaos without a care.

Into the wild, we dance all day,
With twirling petals leading the way.
A path of color calls us near,
To dance in nature's joyful cheer!

Harmonies of the Untamed Earth

In the wild where the grass laughs loud,
Fluffy clouds gather, a whimsical crowd.
They sing with the daisies, bloom the tune,
While ladybugs tap dance beneath the moon.

A yellow fern plays its leafy flute,
A caterpillar struts in a tiny suit.
The grasshoppers click, creating the beat,
Nature's orchestra on a floral street.

As petals unfold, they join in the fun,
Who knew each blossom could dance and run?
A symphony blooms, with each playful prance,
In this concert of colors, let's take a chance!

So grab a flower, let's make some noise,
Join the vibrant band, oh what joy!
With petals as instruments, we'll sing and we'll sway,
In this untamed earth, let's laugh all day!

Vivacious Petals in the Wind

Petals dance like they know the beat,
On a breeze that lifts their tiny feet.
Bumblebees buzz with a silly glee,
Playing tag with each daisy and brie.

Silly stalks twirl, in a flowery waltz,
With the sun as their judge, oh what a vault!
Ladybugs laugh, their spots all askew,
As petals whisper, "Join in, won't you?"

Grass tickles toes in a playful tease,
While butterflies flutter with utmost ease.
Dandelions puff with a cheeky sigh,
As they send fluffy wishes up high.

Pansies roll their eyes at the orchard's tone,
"Oh, look at those roses, they think they're alone!"
Laughter erupts in the field so bright,
Where colors collide in sheer delight.

Revelry of the Vibrant Meadow

In fields of laughter, the colors collide,
Where daisies giggle and sunflowers bide.
A mischief of petals, all striped and spotted,
Whispering secrets, the bold and the spotted.

A clumsy snail slips on dewy ground,
Rolling over, laughter is all around.
Each clover sways with a subtle jest,
As butterflies flaunt in their vibrant best.

Chasing the breeze, a bee takes a sip,
From a cup of nectar, he slips and flips.
"Hey, watch it!" he yells, as he buzzes in flight,
While the poppies giggle, oh what a sight!

Under the sun, a celebration grows,
With laughter and dance, in garden clothes.
Nature's own comedy, a scene so grand,
In the vibrant meadow, where we all stand.

Petals in the Breeze

Petals twirl in a merry-go-round,
Swaying to tunes that can barely be found.
Wiggly worms do the cha-cha in dirt,
While grasses laugh, tossing their green skirts.

A butterfly slips, on its elegant glide,
Turning to talk to the beetle beside.
"Oh dear," says the oxeye, with petals in care,
"Watch out for the wind, it's up to no fare!"

Frogs croak a tune, with a hint of a snort,
In a chorus of giggles, too silly to sport.
The daisies chime in, with a wink and a snicker,
The whole garden's grinning, the laughs just get thicker.

As shadows grow long, the flowers unwind,
Telling wild stories, each flashily blind.
With a twinkle and shimmer, the day takes a bow,
Petals in the breeze, oh we love them now!

Colorful Echoes of Nature

In a garden of hues, where the zinnias peek,
Colors shout laughter, they're charming, not meek.
A poppy declares, with a flamboyant sway,
"Come see my dress, it's the talk of the day!"

Marigolds gossip, with petals aglow,
"Did you hear that? Oh no, there's a crow!"
Glorious daisies roll in the grass,
"Joy's just a wink, as we frolic and pass."

Crickets compose a symphony loud,
While tiny ants form a marching crowd.
In a whirl of colors, a party unfolds,
Where joy is contagious, and fun never molds.

From roses to violets, the laughter will spread,
In echoes of colors, where nature is led.
A tale to remember, as petals are free,
In this canvas of giggles, just wait and you'll see!

The Unexpected Beauty of the Forgotten

In a patch where shadows lay,
A dandelion decided to play.
Waving its yellow head with glee,
Mocking the roses with a snicker, you'll see.

Once ignored but now in sight,
It dances in the fading light.
A rebel in a garden grand,
Creating chaos, never bland.

Who knew that fate would be so sly,
That weeds could share a laugh and sigh?
A daisy with a crooked smile,
Turns the garden into a spoofed aisle.

So raise a toast to the obscure,
In every nook, there's joy for sure.
A laughing flower, bold and bright,
Makes forgotten spots a funny sight.

Flickers of Color in Quiet Corners

In the hidden nooks of the yard,
A purple hue peeked, acting hard.
Whispering secrets to the breeze,
A butterfly giggling with such ease.

A cluster of poppies crept with glee,
Playing hide-and-seek with a busy bee.
Lurking low, they plotted in cheer,
"Let's confuse the gardeners here!"

With petals like crayons tossed around,
They laughed at the chaos they found.
Each vibrant patch a prankster's stunt,
In the corners where the laughter won't blunt.

Neighbors frown, "What a mess!" they say,
But the flowers laugh in their bright ballet.
Who cares if the outcome's not neat?
Life is a giggle, wild and sweet!

Dreams Dashed on Gentle Stalks

A tall tale spun by the wind's breath,
Of daisies dreaming of a noble death.
"I'll be a bouquet," they declared with pride,
Until a roaming cat flopped down and sighed.

Pushed to the side, they pondered their fate,
"Is this how we meet our flowered state?"
Laughter erupted, the breeze took its cue,
These dreams dashed were just moments of blue.

As petals brushed earth, what a sight!
A comedy played in the fading light.
The cat purred loud, a playful thief,
Grabbing dreams quick, but bringing no grief.

So here's to the dreams that don't come true,
They often lead to laughter anew.
In the gardens where humor finds a spark,
Even dashed dreams can leave a mark.

The Joyful Canvas of the Unruly Meadow

In a meadow where the rulebooks lie,
Dandelions laughed as butterflies fly.
Swaying wildly with no care to fit,
Each colorful bloom a charming little wit.

Sunshine spills on every leaf,
Not a flower here hides its belief.
"Let's paint chaos!" they chant with glee,
A canvas of color for all to see.

Forget the tidy rows and plans,
This riot of color is where joy stands.
With a playful wink, the wind gives chase,
As flowers frolic in this open space.

Oh, what fun in a jumbled hue,
Each petal tells a story new.
In the joyful throng, there's much to sing,
In the unruly beauty, we find our spring.

The Charm of Blooms Unchained

In gardens bright, the petals prance,
A bee's sweet dance, a clumsy chance.
With floppy hats and sunbeams bright,
They sing to clouds, oh what a sight!

The tulips argue, who is best?
The roses pout, they feel distressed.
And daisies chuckle at the fuss,
While wishing someone'd ride the bus!

Petunias wear their polka dots,
While sunflowers tie up all the knots.
With laughter sprouting everywhere,
It's hard to breathe and find some air!

So if you wander through this land,
Prepare for giggles, just as planned.
Where petals dance and colors play,
Embrace the whimsy of the day!

Canvas of Nature's Joy

In hues of pink, a canvas beams,
With dandelions sharing dreams.
Petals prattling, colors bright,
They giggle softly in the light.

The violets whisper cheeky things,
Like gossips pulled by floral strings.
Each stem a jester, green and sly,
They catch a breeze, they twist and fly!

With marigolds in funny hats,
And thistles playing with the rats.
Their laughter echoes through the trees,
Each playful gust a gentle tease.

So paint the world with petals bold,
A tale of fun and whimsy told.
In nature's art, let's lose our cares,
For joy is woven everywhere.

Dancing Daisies Under the Moon

Under the moon, the daisies twirl,
In ruffled skirts, they spin and whirl.
With tiny feet that tap so light,
They shimmy through the starry night.

The frogs are croaking, keeping beat,
While nightingales provide the heat.
The lilies sway in rhythm, too,
It's quite a party, who knew?

With lanterns hung from branches high,
The fireflies wink, oh me, oh my!
Each bloom a dancer, full of glee,
Just watch them go, a sight to see!

So join the jig, the floral parade,
In batches bright, their joy portrayed.
As petals cheer and laughter spills,
The night is young, with endless thrills!

Enchanted Glades of Sweet Fragrance

In hidden glades, the scent invites,
Where blossoms plot and share delights.
A clover wee, a sneaky prank,
Has all the flowers in a rank.

The lilacs spread their gossip wide,
While peonies try to play the guide.
Rambunctious petals, bold and bright,
Unruly blooms, a joyful sight!

The jasmine giggles, ticklish air,
With honeysuckle in a snare.
Oh, what a ruckus! What a fun!
Each fragrant whim to outdo one!

So wander deep where laughter grows,
In fragrant fields, among the shows.
Let petals dance upon your skin,
For joy in blooms will always win!

Notes from the Hidden Gardens

In the shade where daisies sing,
A snail wears glasses just like a king.
Bees argue over who has the best buzz,
While butterflies sip nectar with a cheerful fuzz.

A gopher wears a tiny hat,
While hedgehogs laugh at the old tomcat.
Lillies dance in the light of day,
As chipmunks juggle their nuts in play.

Sprouts wiggle where the mud pops loud,
In a parade, they gather, a colorful crowd.
Even the grasshoppers hop with flair,
Bringing giggles to the fragrant air.

The gardener joins in their spree,
Trying to waltz with a bumblebee.
As petals swirl in a gusty breeze,
Who knew gardens had such a tease?

Vibrant Chaos Among the Thorns

Thorns wear crowns made of bright blooms,
While ladybugs practice their dance moves.
Rabbits in suits plot their next trick,
Underneath a sunlit, prancing stick.

A coriander plant tells silly jokes,
As bumblebees chuckle and take to pokes.
The roses argue about who's more sweet,
While daisies giggle on nimble feet.

A butterfly steals nectar without a care,
Winking at the grass with a breezy flare.
As mushrooms gather to throw a feast,
They toast to the sun, at least to say the least.

The wind carries giggles through every leaf,
As plants rejoice—beyond all belief!
In this wacky patch of glee and mirth,
We find that chaos is fun to unearth!

Tapestry of Nature's Fancies

In a meadow stitched with threads of light,
A squirrel wears a cloak of sheer delight.
With daisies dangling from his tiny ears,
He jigs through grasses with no fears.

The daisies twirl and call him 'mate',
While butterflies tease, saying, "You're late!"
Beetles on bikes race the wind uphill,
While mushrooms sip on dew, all still.

A laughing vine sneaks up a tree,
Just to whisper sweet jokes, carefree.
Tulips giggle with each graceful bow,
Confetti from petals falling now.

In this colorful scene, the fun won't cease,
As critters gather and share a piece.
Life's a riot—just take a look,
Nature's story is the best comic book!

The Hidden Charms of Overgrown Fields

In fields where secrets flutter by,
A butterfly paddles up in the sky.
Grasshoppers wear striped pajamas at night,
And giggle at fireflies glowing bright.

A sleepy owl spins tales with a wink,
While ants debate what to eat and drink.
Sunflowers gossip and stretch so tall,
Sharing rumors with everyone, big and small.

The wind adds music, a tune so spry,
As clouds dance in rhythm—oh me, oh my!
Chasing shadows, they skip and twirl,
Bringing laughter to the earth's gentle whirl.

As night falls, the critters sing their cheers,
With chuckles buzzing through the years.
In this patch of chaos, wait and see,
Nature's laughter is the key to glee!

Intrigues of Pollinators and Petals

A bee with a bowtie, quite dapper, it seems,
Dances from blossom to blossom, with dreams.
"I'll sip on your nectar, dear flower, don't pout,"
But petals just giggle and whisper, "Get out!"

A butterfly flutters, a hat on its head,
"What's that? A free meal?" it slyly then said.
The daisies just snicker, with petals a-shake,
"You'll never be full; you're too thin for a cake!"

The ladybug chuckles, it's quite the charmer,
"I'm here for the aphids; you'll see I'm a farmer!"
But ants are all waiting, with plans of their own,
"You'll find out real soon, here you're out on your own!"

Oh, petals unite in a floral debate,
As creatures conspire to dine and sedate.
In this vibrant shindig, the humor runs deep,
Among all the blooms, a secret to keep!

Chasing Shadows in Flowered Fields

In fields where the colors collide and they gleam,
A squirrel, quite silly, swings through on a beam.
"Excuse me, dear daisies, I'm checking for shade,
Could one of you kindly hop up to invade?"

The tulips are tall, with a stance like a knight,
"Stand back, little critter, we're guarding the light!"
While sunbeams just giggle, they're casting their rays,
And blossoms all murmur, "Oh, what clever plays!"

Then comes along dandelion's jest,
"Hey there, furry critter, you want to contest?"
A tumbleweed tumbles, it rolls in to say,
"Just blow me away, and I'll join in the fray!"

The shadows grow shorter, the laughter runs wild,
In this merry circus, each petal's a child.
They frolic and play in the colorful sun,
Chasing their shadows, oh what silly fun!

The Mirage of Springtime Bliss

In gardens where dreams tickle petals awake,
A jester, a gopher, on jokes they both stake.
"What's green and goes bounce?" asks the gopher with glee,
The daisies erupt, "A hare, can't you see?"

Petals all giggling, the laughter does swell,
As poppies play tricks, casting spells with a yell.
"Oh look at us dance, we're no flowers in lines,
But marionette wonders wrapped up in divine!"

The lavender chuckles, with scent in the air,
"Do tell us your secrets, oh joyful affair!"
The sunbeams just wink, as they lighten the scene,
Where colors burst forth, in a zephyr-like dream.

With blooms all a'twirl, it's a whimsical race,
In this mirage where joys dare to trace.
In springtime's embrace, they all sway and respond,
A petal parade where all nonsense is fond!

Anatrichia Amidst the Petals

Amidst all the petals, a dance of delight,
A creature named Anatrichia took flight.
"I'm here for the fun! Just a giggle, no fuss,
But watch me, dear flowers, I'll make quite a fuss!"

With twirls and with whirls, it twinkled and spun,
The daisies all gasped, "Oh, you're quite the one!"
While roses rolled eyes, their thorns all kept close,
"You may be charming, but be cautious, my dos!"

"I'm fragile, I swear! Just a joke, can't you see?"
Anatrichia giggled, feeling wild and free.
"Watch out for the breeze; it could whisk me away,
But petals can't hold, and I just want to play!"

So round and around, it danced with such glee,
In echoes of laughter, the joy set it free.
Among all the blooms, anatrichia danced,
In a world of whimsy, where spirits enhanced.

The Palette of Forgotten Gardens

In gardens where the daisies laugh,
A pickle grows a leafy mustache,
The roses throw a pink parade,
While carrots wear a bright, green sash.

The sunflowers dance with twisty feet,
They juggle bees with sunny flair,
Each bloom plays its silly tune,
And giggles blossom in the air.

The violets tell the bees a tale,
Of ants that waltz on clover leaves,
While dandelions blow their seeds,
And share their fluff with gossip thieves.

So wander through this painted space,
Where laughter roots are surely found,
In muted tones of crazy blooms,
A tapestry of joy unbound.

Eclectic Blossoms at Dusk

At twilight's brush, the tulips grin,
They wear the moon like a silver cap,
With poppies spinning tales of joy,
While crocus trades his evening nap.

The lavenders break into song,
Each petal sways in rhythmic cheer,
As frisky thymes mimic their moves,
And giggles echo far and near.

Chrysanthemums in flouncy skirts,
Twist and twirl in the gentle wind,
Boots of grass they laugh to wear,
In this ballet, they all are pinned.

With shades of laughter and whimsy spry,
The dusky blooms create delight,
An eclectic show of nature's jest,
As day succumbs to giggly night.

Sunlit Laughter of Meadow Spirits

In the meadow where critters chatter,
Each blade of grass has a funny face,
The daisies giggle and share their jokes,
While butterflies flutter in a wild race.

The clovers prank the passing bees,
'Come try our treacle, sticky and sweet!'
The ladybugs giggle with tiny glee,
As dragonflies tap dance down the street.

When sunlight spills over blooming laughs,
Each sprout joins in a joyful cheer,
A celebration of the funny things,
That grow amidst the grass so dear.

As laughter lingers upon the breeze,
These spirits of joy hum a merry tune,
In the sunlit fields, they spin and sway,
Creating chaos beneath the moon.

Fragments of Floral Daydreams

In a garden of whimsical plots,
Where marigolds wear silly hats,
The snapdragons snicker and tease,
While squirrels play games with acrobatic rats.

Petunias gossip with secret sighs,
Each bloom is a friend with a quirky grin,
And every plant has a tale to share,
Of garden capers that spark with sin.

Pansies pull pranks with unmatched flair,
They swirl in skirts of vibrant hues,
While ivy wraps around the toes,
Of a toad who croaks funny blues.

So tiptoe through these daydreams wild,
Where every petal sings and swings,
In fragments of laughter, bright and bold,
A festival of floral flings.

Serenade of the Swaying Stems

In a garden where giggles bloom,
The petals dance to a playful tune.
Bees wear hats, buzzing with glee,
While butterflies join in, wild and free.

A dandelion with a cheeky grin,
Makes jokes about whiskers and furry kin.
The tulips flap like a vibrant sock,
As they strategize to outwit the clock.

Sunflowers sway with a silly flair,
Throwing shade at anyone who dares.
They swap secrets with the buzzing bees,
And always giggle in the soft breeze.

A wobbly stem loses its charm,
But do not fret, it's just a prank, not harm.
In this whimsical patch, laughter's the key,
Join the dance, be as silly as can be!

Mischief in the Meadow

In a meadow where mischief sprouts,
The rabbits plot, fueled by doubts.
Who will win the race to the moon?
Said a sly turtle with a cheeky tune.

Squirrels chuckle, tossing their acorns,
While giggling flowers wear their thorny adorns.
A wind-borne breeze tickles the grass,
As worms wiggle and giggle, oh what a pass!

A ladybug rolls in the sunshine's glow,
Spilling secrets only daisies know.
With tiny hats made of clover leaves,
They conspire quietly, giggles up their sleeves.

Giddy grasshoppers jump like they're mad,
Their giggles echo, making all glad.
Mischief's afoot, let the fun begin,
In a meadow so merry, all hearts wear a grin!

Chasing Rainbows Amongst Petals

Chasing colors where the flowers grow,
A clumsy bee tripped over a toe.
With petals painted in vibrant hues,
They laugh at the paint that always renews.

A bright bluebird sings with a twist,
Poking fun at the bloom's little mist.
Rainbows hide, just out of sight,
While petals giggle, oh what a delight!

A flower sneezes, sending pollen near,
The butterflies burst out laughing, oh dear!
With each sneeze, clouds join the fun,
As colors blend, oh how they run!

Through petals soft, they race and glide,
With giggles breaking, there's no place to hide.
Chasing rainbows in a fragrant spree,
A whimsical dance 'neath the old oak tree!

Tales from the Unruly Blossom

In a patch of blooms where chaos reigns,
Petals gossip about weathered stains.
A rose with an attitude, oh so bright,
Claims she can outshine everyone's light.

Daisies plot to sway with the breeze,
While lavender buds take silly selfies with ease.
The sun joins in, tickling the leaves,
Swapping tales that make everyone wheeze.

A misfit flower, all out of place,
Wears a crooked grin on its cheeky face.
It tells wild stories of starlit nights,
And moonlit dances under twinkling lights.

Gather 'round for tales spun with laughter,
In a realm where humor's the happily ever after.
Unruly blossoms weave magic and cheer,
Bringing joy in abundance, year after year!

The Delicate Balance of Earth's Whimsy

In a garden where socks lose their pair,
Dancing daisies flaunt without a care.
Worms wear sunglasses, quite in style,
While ants throw parties, oh what a while!

The chubby bees buzz with a tune,
While butterflies glide like a cartoon.
Grasshoppers sing on their leafy stage,
Debating politics, though quite a rage.

The trees gossip about the weather's mood,
While mushrooms chuckle, feeling quite rude.
Twirling petals on a whimsical breeze,
Nature's ballet, sure to please.

As rain drops dance on a happy leaf,
The frogs leap high, unfazed by grief.
In this whimsical chaos, life seems so sweet,
Where mischief and laughter are truly a treat.

Dancing Tails of Sunlit Butterflies

Butterflies flap like they own the space,
Wiggling their tails with a funky grace.
Chasing the sunbeams with quirky delight,
Twisting and turning, they're quite a sight!

With each little bounce, they tease the blooms,
It's a crazy dance in the wilds' rooms.
Grass sways to the rhythm of buzzing songs,
In this concert, nature can't go wrong.

Honeybees join in, a buzzing brigade,
Complaining about their unending trade.
While ladybugs sip on dew drops' cheer,
They toast to the butterflies spreading near.

Wings flutter bright, like a jazzy band,
In the world of blooms, it's truly grand.
While ants march in with a marching beat,
Nature's embrace is a jubilant feat.

The Artistry of Nature's Rebellion

In colors so bold, nature takes a stand,
Painting with mischief, so unplanned.
Roses wear thorns like a crown of pride,
While bushes debate who gets to decide.

Moss grows wild, like hair untamed,
Rambunctious vines are truly famed.
Wild herbs conspire, plotting a scheme,
To mimic the sun in a luscious dream.

Dandelions giggle as they sprout,
With wishes attached, they flit about.
Treasure hunts find lost bits of glee,
In a realm of chaos, they're so carefree.

The trees sway with laughter, sharing the jest,
Telling dragonflies they're truly the best.
In chaos and charm, they find their art,
Nature's rebellious, a cheeky heart.

Where the Wild Things Bloom

In meadows where nonsense takes its flight,
Flowers wear hats, oh what a sight!
Caterpillars juggle with vibrant flair,
As bees in tuxedos sip on sweet air.

Thistles and thorns plot their cheeky spree,
Declaring a party, come one, come thee!
Daisies play hopscotch, having a ball,
While mushrooms high-five, standing so tall.

The breeze whispers secrets, oh what a tease!
While crickets compose their symphonies with ease.
Violet laughter blooms from each tree,
Creating a tapestry, wild and free.

In this riot of colors, the earth wears a grin,
Nature's own gallery, where fun begins.
Join the wild things where joy finds its room,
In the magic of chaos where dreams freely bloom.

Notes of a Wandering Wanderer

In the woods I sing a song,
My compass spins, I drift along.
The squirrels dance, the rabbits prance,
I trip on roots while I take a chance.

The flowers giggle with a flare,
They wiggle and jiggle without a care.
Butterflies wear their fanciest attire,
While I find mud—that's my quagmire!

The breeze whispers secrets of the day,
The world is goofy, in every way.
I chase my hat as it takes flight,
What a sight, it's pure delight!

So here's to mischief, roots, and glee,
I wander well, with all that I see.
With nature's laughter, I'll pacify,
This whimsied heart, I won't deny!

A Tiling of Color Beyond the Trees

Poppies and daisies, a patchwork spread,
I trip on petals, it's like I'm wed.
The birds are loud, they sing and shout,
While I ponder what it's all about.

Colors collide, a painter's dream,
The daisies shout, "We're all a team!"
My jeans are stained, a lovely sight,
As bees buzz by, oh what a flight!

With every step, I dance and twirl,
The sun shines bright, oh what a whirl!
The butterflies tease with a daring flair,
As I trip and tumble, they just stare.

So here I skip, in hues galore,
Lost in laughter, wanting more.
Each petal giggles, every leaf grins,
In this vibrant world, everyone wins!

Hidden Lullabies of the Fields

The tall grass whispers, a soft embrace,
As I tumble down, oh what a chase!
Crickets serenade with their buzzing croon,
While I chase fireflies under the moon.

The daisies hum a sweet little tune,
Their happy faces greet the moon.
I try to sing, but sound like a crow,
And the flowers laugh, they steal the show!

I wave at the breeze, it tickles my nose,
Each rustle is laughter, as the night glows.
The stars join in with a twinkle and wink,
While I lose my step, but don't even think!

So come join the chorus, a field's sweet sound,
In this hidden lullaby, joy is found.
With every giggle in the dusky light,
Our hearts will dance through the quiet night!

Rainbow Revelations in a Meadow

In a meadow bright, colors collide,
I wander as laughter becomes my guide.
Each blossom waves, a spirited friend,
To frolic and tumble, the fun won't end.

Divine hues giggle, a sight so nice,
Like confetti dropped from heaven's spice.
I try to match their joyful spree,
But find myself stuck in a raspberry.

With every step, I leap and sway,
The colors tease—come out and play!
Oh, daisies, roses, bask in the sun,
What a splendid day, oh what fun!

So here's to laughter, shades bright and bold,
In this meadow of joy, let the stories unfold.
With each silly dance, we color the air,
In our rainbow world, with love to share!

Secrets of the Colorful Exuberance

In gardens where the daisies tease,
Bees dance around with the utmost ease.
Petals whisper secrets, oh so sly,
While butterflies giggle as they flutter by.

Sunflowers wear hats, oh what a sight!
Twirling in breezes, pure delight.
The colors clash, a paintbox spills,
Nature's confetti gives us thrills.

Tulips in loafers, oh what a pair,
Strutting through meadows without a care.
Laughter erupts from the bushes nearby,
As critters join in and let out a sigh.

Amidst this chaos, joy's rhythm sways,
Who knew the blooms liked to play?
In a show of hues, bright smiles gleam,
Nature's carnival, a whimsical dream.

A Symphony of Unrestrained Blooms

Cardinals hum tunes from blossom to leaf,
While roses wiggle, beyond belief.
With petals twirling in the sun's embrace,
Nature's orchestra, a merry place.

Daffodils chat about their old friends,
While wisteria giggles and twists and bends.
Violets in skirts spin with glee,
In this floral party, wild and free.

Dandelions float like fluffy dreams,
Tickling the grasses with their schemes.
A pollen parade, a cheerful show,
Every bloom joins in, oh what a flow!

Under the moonlight, mischief unfolds,
With moonflowers whispering tales bold.
In this garden bound by laughter's tune,
The blooms revel under the cheeky moon.

The Playful Tangle of Vines

Climbing up fences, the ivy climbs high,
Swaying and laughing as squirrels pass by.
With tendrils that twist in a spirited dance,
Every vine seems to seize the chance.

Wisteria hugs the oldest tree,
Scheming and plotting quite sneakily.
While broccoli gives a sage nod,
Proving that greens can be charmingly odd.

Pumpkins roll in a joking parade,
Under the sun, they're unafraid.
Their orange coats gleam, such a jest,
In the game of life, they're feeling blessed.

So come take a stroll, let laughter bloom,
In this tangled world, dismiss the gloom.
For among twisted vines and leaf's embrace,
Nature's mischief whirls in a playful space.

Ecstasy Amongst the Herbs

In pots of thyme, there's a cheeky cheer,
As basil hums tunes that you want to hear.
Oregano winks, "Let's spice up the day!"
While parsley prances in a lively display.

Mint sprigs giggle with the wind's soft kiss,
Making mojitos of sheer bliss.
Rosemary claps, "Life can be grand!"
With a dash of humor, it takes a stand.

Chives rise tall, with a cultured poise,
Their snickers are hushed, but they sure make noise.
A seasoning dance, so boldly unchained,
In this herbaceous party, there's nothing contained.

Join this communion of fragrant delight,
Where laughter lingers both day and night.
In gardens of flavor, such joy we find,
Herbs celebrate whimsy, with heart and mind.

www.ingramcontent.com/pod-product-compliance
Lightning Source LLC
Chambersburg PA
CBHW071853160426
43209CB00003B/542